CAUSE TO PAUSE

BOBBIE J. GULLEY

DEDICATED

To the wonderful family members who has walked along my life's path: Lottie, a loving and entertaining Grandmother. Earlie and Mattie, my parents who were strong in spirit, love of family and loyalty.

CONTENTS

ACKNOWLEDGEMENTS

Parents, Teachers, Mentors, Coaches, Counselors and Friends who make the effort to spend quality time with children, kids, tweens and teenagers to help them through the different years and stages of being a child, a teenager and finally an adult. You do your best to encourage young people to do their best in school, hold onto their faith, keep in fellowship with the Holy Trinity and to continue to look up for Jesus, our returning King.

CAUSE TO PAUSE

By

Bobbie J. Gulley

Theme: Distractions that can sometime invade the Teenager's Christian walk.

Church Year Season: Anytime

Suggested Uses:
1. An opportunity for the Youths in Church to get involved in Church Ministry.
2. Another way to give an invitation for the lost to accept the Lord Jesus Christ.

Scripture References and/or Quotes: I Peter 5:8; (Proverbs 14:14); Acts 18:9; Psalm 73:3; Psalm 128:1; James 1:8; Psalm 119:98; I Corinthians 14:33; Isaiah 40:31; Psalm 51:12; I Corinthians 14:1; Matthew 16:26; James 4:4; Proverbs 18:24; (Matthew 10:32); John 16:13; Psalm 51:10; Psalm 51:7; Psalm 51:9; Psalm 51:1-2; Matthew 28:20; (Revelation 9:20-21); (Matthew 13:42); Ephesians 5:16

Synopsis: People and the world affect our walk with Jesus, especially when we are young and vulnerable. We have to be careful in how we are stepping.

Cast Breakdown: (58)

32 Males
26 Females

PROPS & COSTUMES

Partitions to form left and right side walls.

-Left side, Rear, and Right side background—with Side walls and Left and Right front Partitions to make the Entrance and Exit.

Left & Right Cover Partitions—must be able to slide across Stage to hide the Props before Performance begins.

-Partitions Covering—should cover the left side, rear, and right side Partitions.

Partitions Covering Items:

-Paper Cutouts of Question marks and Exclamation points.

-Biblical Pictures, Posters, Paintings or a Covering showing images of thing that Teens like to do (i.e., skateboarding).

-Paper Cutouts of all the different Names of the Social Media used by Teenagers.

-Paper Cutouts of Printed Words—*(Acceptance, Abstinence, Courage, Dating, Faith, Forgiveness, Grace, Holiness, Individuality, Love, Mercy, Peer Pressure, Reconciliation, Redemption, Repent Now, Salvation)*

Partitions Covering Note: Director should ask Cast members if there are any other Words, Social Media, Electronic devices of other device that is popular among their group. If some of them are appropriate, then they may be displayed on the Partition Cover and/or among the other Props.

-Make sure the Props do not **crowd** the Stage or take away any attention from any Cast Member.

1—Snare Drum or full Drum set with sticks

2—Stands for Guitars—must have cross bar to hand headphones.
    1—Acoustic Guitar
    1—Electric Guitar

1—Keyboard with Stand
2—Sets of colorful Sneakers—different types and brands
2—Sets of the latest Headphones or two empty boxes showing their images.

Boxes—empty—showing the latest/newest gaming and other devices,
    1—X-Box
    1—PlayStation
    1—WiiU
    1—Drone
    1—Gaming machine
    1—Laptop

A Low or small barrier should be made near the edge of the Stage to prevent the Hospital beds from accidently rolling off the Stage.

1—Chair—portable but comfortable

Medical Equipment
    1—Hospital beds with IV Poles—each with Drip and blood bags attached.
        -Blood for the bags will be made with water and red dye.
        -Any other equipment/cables/tubes, associated with critical care.
        -Anything that can be connected to the Beds so that everything can be rolled in together by the LPNs and Nurses when they roll in the Beds.
    1—Hospital Chart—(attachment on beds to hold it.)

'The Machines'
    1—Heart monitor machine
    1—Defibrillator—for use on YOUTH 2
    1—Blood pressure and Drip machines

Medical Note: The S-Recordings will be used as the sound of 'the Machines' therefore they do not need to be plugged in.

Bed Note: One Hospital bed may be used as long as everything is attached for the condition of the 'Patients.'
    -The 'Rear' side of the bed on Stage is the side not facing the audience.

Equipment Note: In pre-Youth and Youth 2's appearance on Stage, 'the Machines' rolled in, will be any other Medical equipment that should be attached to the Patient or the Hospital bed that is needed for critical care patients. See Stage and Scene Instructions.

YOUTH & YOUTH 2
    2—Oxygen masks
    2—Hospital gowns
    4—White sheets
    4—Blankets
        -Bandages for wrists of YOUTH

YOUTH 2
    -Bandages for part of her face and head
    1—Bottle of Red paint for blood stain
    1—Tubing Device with Pumper
        -The Device will allow YOUTH 2 to squeeze a small amount of red dye into the side of the bandages that is facing the audience at the right time.

-The Device should be angled under her neck and head but not be able to be seen by the audience.

All NURSES + DOCTOR
    4—Stethoscopes
    4—Ink pens

GUARD & GUARD 2
    1—Belt with ammo & gun holsters.
    1—Plastic Gun.

T-PRISONER
    1—Set of Prison Shackles for wrists and ankles.

DESIRE
    -iPhone, 7" tablet, Headphones or any other popular Teen electronic devices that are hand-carried—at least 2 of the devices.

FALLEN
    -Make-up Kit—for black eyes because of her broken nose.
    -Large temporary tattoo for her neck.
    -Bandages for her face and broken nose.
    -Walking Cast for broken foot.

LIGHTING
1-2—Spotlights for highlighting Center Stage.
    -Adjustable lights to highlight and fade to black instead of just instantly turning them off.
Stage lights—to illuminate up entire stage.

SOUND
Face Mikes—for the Cast, if enough is available. If not, use Remote, Standing and/or Hangings Mikes.
    -Remote mikes for each SOLOIST and CHOIR member to use.
    -Hanging Mikes—needed, if not enough Remote mikes for the CHOIR.

2-3—Standing mikes, if used for the Non-singing Cast.

Hanging Mikes—if used, will be place in strategic places on Stage to ensure sound is uniform and clear to audience.

NOTE: U-SPEAKERS—Their voices must sound as though they are speaking from above the audience.

Vocal Recording: Hymns to be played in a loop while audience is finding their seats:
Hymns #413, "Turn Your Eyes upon Jesus," #415, "Room at the Cross," and #416, "Let Jesus Come into Your Heart."

Music for Hymns sung by SOLOISTS and CHOIR:
Hymns #508, "Have Faith in God," Hymn #476, "Be Strong in the Lord," #317, "Only Trust Him" and #506,"In Christ Alone (My Hope Is Found)" and #65, "Just When I Needed Him Most."

Operator(s) for S-Recordings = SR Operators: They must know how to operate recording equipment to make sure that:
1. That all Sound and Voice Recordings are recorded on quality devices.
2. That at least one other Back-up Recording of all Recordings be made as insurance for Performance.
3. That all the Recordings *(Sound/YDR/USD)* are turned on, volume adjusted and turned off and on again in perfect timing.
4. When S-Recording #1 and #2 are turned off at the end of each YDR, S-Recording #3 must be ready to be turned on in a second.

YOUTH Dialogue Recording = **YDR**
YOUTH 2 Dialogue Recording = **YDR 2**

YOUTH and YOUTH 2 Dialogue Recordings:
-The Recorded Dialogues will ensure the consistency of their voices.
-Make two (2) Recordings of their Dialogues as backup.
-The Recorded Dialogues will be made by the Actors who will be lying in the Hospital Beds on Stage, if possible.
-Both Youths will record their dialogue as soon as they have perfected their lines.

U-SPEAKERS Dialogues —*(USD Recordings)*: *(If needed)* This is to ensure consistence of voices and/or as a backup if U-SPEAKER Cast members are not able to perform. U-SPEAKERS Dialogues should be recorded in sets.

Sound Recordings:
-1—Recording—*(S-Recording #1)*—The Heartbeat sound of someone who is recovering from a drug overdose.
-1—Recording—*(S-Recording #2)*— The sound of Blood pressure or Heart monitor machines.
-1—Recording—*(S-Recording #3)*—Alarm going off to signal something wrong with Pressure or Heart monitor.

-1—Recording—*(S-Recording #4)*—The heartbeat sound of someone who is trying to recover from surgery from a gunshot wound to the head.
    -1—Recording—*(S-Recording #5)*—Sound of the Heart monitor going flat at the end of *S-Recording #3.*

Sound Recordings: Must be able to adjust the volume of #1 and #2.

S-Recording #6: If a Recording is needed for the sound of the defibrillator paddles being applied.

NOTE: Sound Recordings #1 and #2: Must be able to adjust the volume so when it is lowered, audience may clearly hear both YDR. Heartbeat and 'the Machines' should be heard throughout both Youths' Dialogues.

SETTING

Position the Partitions to form a background that consist of Center Partitions and other Partitions to form left and right side walls.

Place the other Partitions to form side walls and an Entrance and an Exit opening.

Position the Sliding Cover Partitions in front of all the other Partitions to hide the Scene.

Attach the Covering to cover the center and side Partitions then decorate the Covering.

Randomly post on the Partitions Covering: Biblical Pictures, Posters, Paintings or images of thing that Teens like to do and/or may want to display.

Then post among the above things, the Cutouts of the Question marks, Exclamation points, the Cutouts of all the different Names of the Social Media used by Teenagers plus the Cutouts of the listed Printed Words.

Place the Snare Drum or full Drum set with sticks in front of the left Partitions.

Place the Sets of colorful Sneakers sideway at the bottom part of the Drum set.

Place the Guitar Stands, with the Acoustic and Electric Guitars in front of the center Partitions.
    -Place one set of Headphones on one of the Guitar Stands.

Place the Keyboard with Stand in front of right Partitions.
    -Place one set of Headphones on the Keyboard.

If any other Teen-related Props are added to the Stage:
       -Make sure that they are placed in relation to the other Props.
Ensure that there is sufficient walking space between the Props and that no Prop is blocking the Entrance and Exit areas.
       -Ensure that additional Props do not crowd the Stage or block the Entry or Exit of Cast members.
       -Also, all Props must not prevent the close assembly of the Cast behind the mikes at the end of the Program.

All three Standing Mikes are positioned center Stage in front of the Props. Adjust them to cover the heights of the shortest to the tallest Cast member.

If Hanging Mikes are used then position them so that they are not seen by the audience.
       -Make sure that the Mikes are placed in strategic places on Stage to ensure sound is uniform and clear to audience especially for the Front Cast members if not enough Remote mikes are available.

Front Stage Space Note:
       -Make sure that there is enough space for the Chair to be placed so that it and NURSE 3 is outside of the range of the Spotlights until it is time for her to get up.
       -Make sure there is enough room in front of them so that Front Cast can enter, stand and exit without being too close to the edge of the Stage.
       -Also make sure that there is enough room in front for the Hospital beds to be rolled and for the Medical Cast to stand near edge without falling off the Stage.

Designated a spot for PASTOR to stand and receive people during the Invitation.

Remove all chalk marks/tapes after final rehearsal.

After everything is in place, roll the Covering Partitions across the Stage to hide the Props and leave until Performance.

CAST OF CHARACTERS

GREETER	Male, Age 13-16, Attire: Dark blue vest and slacks, white shirt, dark blue tie, black belt and shoes
SOLOIST	Male
CHOIR	3 Males, 3 Females
PM	(2) 1 Male, 1 Female, Age 13-16, Partitions Movers, Attire for both: black Polo shirt, slacks, belt and sneakers
SPEAKER	Male, Age 30+
SPEAKER 2	Female, Age 30+
SPEAKER 3	Male, Age 30+
JUMPER	Male, Age 15-19
ENVY	Female, Age 14-19, Attire: Plain blouse, blue jeans, belt and sneakers
SOLOIST 2	Female
SPEAKER 4	Female
ANGRY	Female, Age 13-19
CONFUSED	Male, Age 17-19, Spiked hair, Attire: Jeans, shirt, sneakers
LPN	Male
LPN 2	Female
YOUTH	Male, Age 16-19, Attire: Hospital gown worn over pullover shirt, short pants and socks
NURSE	Female, Age 24-30
NURSE 2	Male, Age 30-35

NURSE 3	Female, Age 35+
U-SPEAKER	Male, Age 13-14
U-SPEAKER 2	Female, Age 13-14
TIRED	Female, Age 15-19
JOY	Male, Age 15-19
SOLOIST 3	Female
GUARD	Male, Age 30+, Attire: Prison Guard uniform with patches and badges, black boots
GUARD 2	Male, Age 30+, Attire: Same as GUARD.
T-PRISONER	Male, Age 15-19, Attire: Prisoner uniform, sneakers
SPEAKER 5	Male, Age 25+
SPEAKER 6	Female, Age 25+
DESIRE	Female, Age 14-19
POPULAR	Female, Age 15-19
B-TEEN	Male, Age 16-19
B-TEEN 2	Female, Age 16-19
HURT	Male, Age 13-19
SPEAKER 7	Male, Age 15-19
SPEAKER 8	Female, Age 15-19
SOLOIST 4	Male
CRIED	Female, Age 16-19

FALLEN	Female, Age 16-19, Two different color tinted hair, Large temporary tattoo on neck, Large bandage on one side of face, bruises on the other side, bandage over nose, one black eye, bandaged left hand, Foot cast on left or right foot. Attire: Trendy teen Outfit, one black boot with bright colored shoe laces on foot that is not in cast.
RAN	Male, Age 15-19, Attire: Football jersey, jeans, belt, sneakers
LONELY	Male, Age 13-19
U-SPEAKER 3	Female, Age 15-19
U-SPEAKER 4	Male, Age 15-19
YOUTH 2	Female, Age and Attire is the same as YOUTH.
DOCTOR	Male, Age 35+, Attire: White medical Jacket, dark blue shirt and slacks, dark/light blue tie, black belt and shoes
SPEAKER 9	Male, Age 15-17
SPEAKER 10	Female, Age 17-19
SPEAKER 11	Male, Age 17-19
SOLOIST 5	Male
PASTOR	Male, Church Pastor, Attire: Dark Gray 2-piece suit, white shirt, dark gray and black striped tie, black belt and shoes

Cast Note: SR Operators must practice with Cast to ensure the Recordings are played at the right moments.

The word Patient(s) is sometimes used to identified YOUTH and YOUTH 2.

All Cast members must have strong and clear voices.

U-SPEAKERS are not on Stage but are situated in a place that is not near any noise source.

GREETER, PM, SOLOISTS, CHOIR, SPEAKERS, LPNS, NURSES, DOCTOR, B-TEENS and PASTOR are considered **Front Cast** because they will either stand or move in front of the mikes and close to the edge of the Stage.

All other Cast members will stand behind the mikes.

YOUTH and YOUTH 2's Beds are to be placed in front of the Mikes.

Name Abbreviations:

SR Operators = Sound Recording   T-PRISONER =Teen Prisoner
U-SPEAKERS = Unseen   B-TEENS = Blaming

Director Note for Assembly: Director may make the decision for YOUTH 2 to reenter with other Cast members at Assembly. Not having her there may show that she did not make it.

SOLOISTS & CHOIR positions on Stage are:
-CHOIR members (M/F/M) — SOLOIST — CHOIR members (F/M/F).

SOLOIST & CHOIR Members' Note: No Robes, no Sneakers or boots will be worn by them.

SOLOIST Ages & Attire: 13-19
-Males—Dark blue shirt, slacks & shoes or black shoes, white/dark blue striped tie, white vest & belt.
-Females—Dark blue dress, leggings & shoes or black shoes, white dangling earrings, necklace and sash.

CHOIR Members' Attire:
-Males—Light blue shirt, slacks, white/dark blue striped tie, black belt & shoes, dark blue vest.
-Females—Light blue dress, dark blue dangling earrings, necklace, sash, leggings & shoes or black shoes.

SPEAKERS Attire:
-Male: White shirt, green vest, slacks, white/green striped tie, black belt and shoes.
-Female: Green dress or outfit and leggings, white and green earrings, white necklace, sash/belt and shoes.

U-SPEAKERS Attire:
   -Male Attire: Dark blue shirt, slacks, shoes, white tie and belts.
   -Female Attire: Dark blue outfit, leggings, shoes, white earrings, sash/belt.

LPN/LPN 2 Note: Ages: 20-25
   -Attire for both male and female: Hospital uniforms plus footwear.

NURSES Note:
   -Attire for all three: Nurse Uniforms plus stethoscopes and other items usually carried by them.
   -Nurse Cast members must be familiar with what to do to critical injured patients when medical alarms goes off.

Attire for Cast Members with no Attire listed: Casual/Trendy Teenager clothing/outfits but modest in style, design and length. *(Polo shirts, regular or khaki slacks, buttoned blouses, no form or tight fitting slacks, dresses or skirts)* Sneakers may be worn with some outfits.

All Attire for Cast members must be modest in styling.

Attire NOTE: All Liked-Attire for CHOIR members and SPEAKERS must have the same formal shade of color and style to include accessories and shoes for each gender.

2-piece Suit = Suit coat and slacks.

Shoes/Sneakers/Boots Note: All **Shoes** are shoes worn with formal-type clothing. **Exceptions**: PM and other Cast members' whose Attire list sneakers, boots or other footwear.

No bright colored clothing for PASTOR.

Additional Attire Information for all Cast:
   -Cast Members' Attire colors and style to include accessories, must not take the focus away from what they are saying or doing.
   -All Attire will be ironed and modest—No wrinkled clothing.
   -All body and clothing accessories must not be reflective.
   -No Face piercing or visible tattoos.
   -Females may accessorize with other jewelry but the items must not overwhelm or distract from the outfit.
   -No Form or tight fitting clothing.
   -No bright colored clothing—unless otherwise stated.

-All Shirts, dresses and blouses are long sleeved—unless otherwise listed.

-All shirts will be tucked into slacks.

-All slacks are to be of 'Suit' material.

-No sagging slacks

-All slacks, pants and jeans are to be worn with a belt.

-No Overly bright colored: shirts, slacks, dresses, skirts or shoes.

-No Cut-off jeans or pants.

-No Cuts or rips in any clothing.

-No safety pins or any other liked items will be clearly visible on clothing.

-No Tee shirts or any other shirt or blouse with wording or graphics

-The colors of all sneakers must not be too bright so that they are distracting to the audience.

-Watches—black wristbands

-Bracelets—non-reflective

-No spike or heels over 2 inches for all footwear—unless otherwise listed.

CAUSE TO PAUSE

ACT ONE

SCENE ONE

BEFORE THE PLAY BEGINS AND AS THE AUDIENCE TAKE THEIR SEATS, PLAY THE VOCAL HYMNS RECORDING REPEATEDLY.

ONE MINUTE BEFORE THE START OF THE PROGRAM, STOP THE RECORDING.

THE ENTRANCE IS ON THE LEFT AND THE EXIT IS ON THE RIGHT. STAGE DIRECTIONS ARE FROM THE AUDIENCE'S VIEW.

FRONT OF STAGE—IS THE AREA IN FRONT OF THE SLIDING COVER PARTITIONS.

THE FIRST STANDING MIKE IS THE ONE CLOSEST TO THE ENTRANCE AND THE THIRD MIKE IS THE ONE NEAREST TO THE EXIT.

ONE PM WILL ENTER FROM ENTRANCE AND THE OTHER ONE WILL ENTER FROM THE EXIT TO ROLL AWAY THE COVERING PARTITIONS. WHEN INSTRUCTED, THEY WILL ROLL THE PARTITIONS BACK INTO PLACE.

MAKE SURE THAT REMOTE MIKES ARE TURNED OFF WHEN NOT USED BY CAST.

CHECK AND MAKE SURE THAT THE SPOTLIGHTS WHEN TURNED ON FOR THE NURSES AND BOTH YOUTHS, ONLY SPOTLIGHTS THEM, THE BEDS AND 'THE MACHINES.'

MAKE SURE THAT THERE IS ENOUGH SPACE FOR THE CHAIR TO BE PLACED SO THAT IT AND NURSE 3 IS OUTSIDE OF THE RANGE OF THE LIGHTS UNTIL IT IS TIME FOR HER TO GET UP.

CAST WILL ENTER FROM THE ENTRANCE AND EXIT THROUGH THE EXIT UNLESS DIRECTED OTHERWISE.

CAST MEMBERS WILL NOTE THEIR ENTRY AND EXIT POINTS AND WILL ENTER AND EXIT IN ORDER.

GREETER, LPNS, YOUTHS, NURSES AND DOCTOR WILL ENTER FROM THE ENTRANCE AND EXIT THROUGH THE ENTRANCE.

ALL GUARDS AND T-PRISONER WILL ENTER FROM THE EXIT AND EXIT BACK THROUGH THE EXIT.

NORMAL INTERVALS OF CAST MEMBERS ENTERING ARE THREE SECONDS AFTER THE PREVIOUS MEMBER HAVE EXITED.

EACH CAST MEMBER WILL WALK NORMAL ONTO THE STAGE (*UNLESS DIRECTED OTHERWISE*) AND EXIT THE SAME WAY. NO RUSHING ONTO OR OFF THE STAGE.

ALL CAST MEMBERS WHO ARE INSTRUCTED TO ENTER TOGETHER WILL ENTER IN ORDER. PLUS, WHILE SPEAKING THEIR DIALOGUE, CAST MEMBERS (*OTHER THAN CHOIR*) WHO ENTER OR STAND TOGETHER WILL FREQUENTLY LOOK AT EACH OTHER AS THOUGH CONVERSING WITH EACH OTHER AS THEY SPEAK TO THE AUDIENCE.

ALL CAST MEMBERS WILL MAKE SURE THAT THE VOLUME ON THEIR PHONES AND ANY OTHER ELECTRONIC DEVICES ARE ON MUTE BEFORE ENTERING BACKSTAGE.

DIRECTOR MUST CONSULT WITH LOCAL HOSPITAL PERSONNEL TO MAKE SURE THAT THE EQUIPMENT BROUGHT ON STAGE WITH THE "PATIENT' IS IN ACCORDING WITH HIS AND HER CONDITION.

DIRECTOR MUST CONSULT WITH LOCAL HOSPITAL STAFF PERSONNEL TO ENSURE THAT THE LPNS, NURSES AND DOCTOR ARE MOVING AROUND THE 'PATIENTS' PROCEDURE-WISE.

DIRECTOR MAY MODIFY SCENE INSTRUCTIONS TO CONFORM WITH REGULAR HOSPITAL PROCEDURES.

ALL NURSES PLUS THE DOCTOR WILL PRACTICE AND BE VERY FAMILIAR WITH WHAT TO DO DURING HOSPITAL PROCEDURES OF ALARMS GOING OFF, PATIENTS GOING INTO CARDIAC ARREST AND APPLYING THE DEFIBRILLATOR PADS.

LPNS AND NURSES WILL PRACTICE ROLLING BEDS WITH SOMEONE ON THEM TO CENTER STAGE SO THAT THEY WILL SMOOTHLY MANEUVER THE BEDS ON STAGE.

LPNS AND NURSES WILL ROLL BEDS WITH YOUTH AND YOUTH 2 IN THEM IN FRONT OF THE MIKES TO CENTER STAGE. THEY ALSO MUST MAKE SURE THAT THE BEDS' BRAKES ARE SET SO THAT THE BEDS DO NOT ROLL OFF THE STAGE.

ALL LPNS, NURSES PLUS THE DOCTOR MUST PRACTICE THEIR MOVEMENTS AROUND 'THE PATIENTS' AND THE HOSPITAL BED SO THAT THEY DO NOT BUMP INTO OR GET INTO EACH OTHER WAY.

ALL LPNS AND NURSES WILL MAKE TWO APPEARANCES.

NURSES 'CHECKING THE PATIENT'—WILL DO WHATEVER IT IS THAT THEY DO TO PATIENTS AFTER THEY ARE PLACED IN A CRITICAL CARE AREA.

FOR YOUTH 2, NURSE 3 WILL REMAIN ON STAGE TO SHOW HOW CRITICAL YOUTH 2'S CONDITION IS.

YOUTH AND YOUTH 2 WILL NOT SPEAK BUT THEIR RECORDINGS WILL BE USED WHILE THEY ARE ON STAGE.

YOUTH AND YOUTH 2 (SEE DIRECTOR NOTE) WILL REENTER AT CAST ASSEMBLY STILL WEARING THEIR HOSPITAL GOWNS PLUS SNEAKERS.

DESIRE MUST KEEP IN MIND THAT SHE IS BRINGING SOMETHING ON STAGE AND/OR HOLDING SOMETHING WHILE SPEAKING.

T-PRISONER WILL PRACTICE ENTERING AND EXITING STAGE WHILE WEARING THE SHACKLES.

T-PRISONER WILL REENTER AT CAST ASSEMBLY STILL WEARING HIS WRIST AND FOOT SHACKLES.

FALLEN WILL PRACTICE ENTERING AND EXITING THE STAGE WHILE WEARING THE CAST ON HER FOOT. ALSO, SHE MUST BE BALANCE ENOUGH TO LIFT THE FOOT WITH CAST UP FOR TWO SECONDS WITHOUT FALLING OVER.

FALLEN WILL REENTER AT CAST ASSEMBLY STILL WEARING HER FOOT CAST AND BANDAGES.

CAST MEMBERS *(EXCEPT FOR T-PRISONER)* WHO CARRIED ANYTHING ON STAGE WILL NOT BRING IT BACK WITH THEM WHEN THEY ASSEMBLE AT THE END OF THE PERFORMANCE.

ALL CAST MEMBERS WILL SPEAK IN A NORMAL VOICE UNLESS INSTRUCTED TO DO OTHERWISE.

ALL CAST MEMBERS WILL USE HAND EXPRESSIONS, GESTURES OR BODY MOVEMENTS WHEN NECESSARY OR TO MAKE A POINT.

EXCEPT FOR BOTH YOUTHS, ALL CAST MEMBERS WITH *"WORLD—YOU CAUSED"* DIALOGUE WILL POINT TOWARD THE AUDIENCE, AS THEY SPEAK THE FIRST LINE. THEN THEY WILL BRING THEIR HAND BACK TO THEIR SIDE. AT THE END OF THEIR DIALOGUE, THEY WILL AGAIN POINT TOWARD THE AUDIENCE WHEN THEY GET TO THE LAST INDICATED PAUSE AND SPEAK *"WORLD, YOU CAUSED"* LINE. AT THE END OF THAT LINE, THEY WILL BRING THEIR HAND BACK TO THEIR SIDE.

ALL DIALOGUE PAUSES ARE FOR TWO SECONDS UNLESS STATED DIFFERENTLY.

CAST ASSEMBLY IS AT THE END OF THE PERFORMANCE WHERE ALL CAST MEMBERS EXCEPT GREETER WILL REENTER THE STAGE BEFORE PASTOR ENTERS.

EXCEPT FOR GREETER, THE REST OF THE CAST SHOULD PRACTICE ASSEMBLING IN A SEMI-CIRCLE ON STAGE BEHIND THE MIKES FOR THE INVITATION.

(The Stage is dark. The Covering Partitions are in place. When the audience is seated, turn off Vocal Hymns Recording. Wait 10 seconds then turn 1-2 Spotlights on in front of the Cover Partitions at center Stage.

Five seconds later, GREETER will enter and go into the Spotlights.)

GREETER: *(Stretch out hands toward audience.)* Welcome ladies and gentlemen, to our Program. We hope that you will enjoy it. *(Pause)* Before we start, we would ask that you please turn off all electronic or any other devices that may make a sound or show any type of lights so that the Program is not interrupted or be a distraction to the Cast Members. *(Pause)* Thank you and enjoy the Program. *(Exit)*

SPEAKER: There are things in life that cause all of us to step back, sit down, stop in our tracks, or just plain pause.

SPEAKER 2: Sometimes these things can be life threatening, life changing or just plain inconvenient.

SPEAKER 3: How we response to these moment changers, can have an effect on us that can alter the way we live for the rest of our lives.

SPEAKER: Some people say young people today have more pressure than any other generation but I say that today's teenager has the same pressure as their parents did, just in a very different way and at a faster pace.

SPEAKER 2: Because they are young and vulnerable, personal and family problems and social distractions are some of the things that can invade the Christian Teenager's walk with Jesus.

SPEAKER 3: Then as they grow older, there are other things such as decisions that have to be made.

SPEAKER: Decisions like as to what they want to be as an adult. What college to go to; what job to get, where to live; who to marry or not to marry.

SPEAKER 2: Decisions that are harder and harder for young people to make because of the many distractions that flood their lives.

SPEAKER 3: Therefore, they have to be careful how they are walking on the road of life *(Pause)* and in what direction.

SPEAKER: Saved teenagers in our churches, as young people in Christ, especially have to be careful because the Devil would love to trip them up so that they fall, pause or abandon their belief and faith in Jesus.

SPEAKER 2: We have all heard the phase, "The World, the Flesh and the Devil."

SPEAKER 3: And all three of them are the opposite of the commandments, the doctrine and the standards of the Lord Jesus Christ.

SPEAKER: The World wants you to play out your life, not by biblical standards but with the rules its makes up.

SPEAKER 2: And we all know how the desire of our Flesh can override the protests of our minds and hearts. And our Flesh can get us to do things that we never thought that we would ever do.

SPEAKER 3: Unfortunately, for all of us, the Devil was there when Adam and Eve lived in Eden, tempting them to sin.

SPEAKER: And he and his demons have had thousands of years since then to hear every word and watch everything that every child of Adam and Eve, to include us today, say and do.

SPEAKER 2: Therefore, the Devil knows how to work the minds of any generation and he is constantly at work using the World and the Flesh to cause us to abandon the ways of righteousness.

SPEAKER 3: And if any of us Pause in our Christian walk, we become spiritually suspended in thought and action of doing anything in our lives and for the Lord Jesus Christ.

SPEAKER: The Word of God tells each of us to "be vigilant; because your adversary the devil, as a roaring lion, walketh about, seeking whom he may devour."

SPEAKER 2: And if we are not constantly on the lookout, the World, the Flesh and the Devil can easily make us step away from the foot of the Cross and from our close relationship with Christ Jesus.

SPEAKER 3: So at this time, we are asking all who are in their teen years, to give a listen.

SPEAKER: While we give you a glimpse of how some people, things or events may Cause you to Pause.

SPEAKER 2: Oftentimes, in such a way that you may become emotionally, bodily and spiritually unstable.

SPEAKER 3: And we ask that you also take the time to reflect on how you are dealing with something that has Caused you to Pause in your walk with Christ.

SPEAKER: We also will note those who fell so far that they could not get up again.

SPEAKER 2: And how others who fell, found ways to pick themselves up again.

SPEAKER 3: *(Pause)* Let's begin!

(All three SPEAKERS will exit. Three seconds later, JUMPER enters and the rest of the Cast follow in order.)

JUMPER: You—the World Caused me to Pause because I Jumped whenever friends of mine asked me to. I did it because I wanted to continue to be part of the group. My friends are not believers in Christ and they make fun of anyone who says anything about Jesus. In my spiritual weakness, I didn't want to lose them as friends so I jumped at the first chance to n-o-t tell them that they needed to know that Jesus is the only one who can save them from their sins. I became in a sense this undercover Christian which made me miserable. Also, I worried that my friends would go beyond the opportunity to be called by the Holy Spirit. Yet I did nothing. Then the Holy Scriptures revealed to me that "if our gospel be hid, it is hid to them that are lost." I thought I was praying for their salvation but deep in my heart, I was praying for them to be saved so that they would not reject me as a friend. *(Pause)* In Proverbs, it talks about how the backslider's heart is filled with his own ways not God's ways. *(Point to self.)* I ask the Lord to forgive me, because I had become a Backslider. And because I didn't want to stay one, I had to man up to what I had become. I had to decide if I loved Jesus enough to face being ostracized by my friends and to do what Jesus has called me to do, *(Bring hand down.)* which is to witness to them and to pray earnestly for them to be saved for Christ's sake. *(Pause)* The Apostle Paul was told by Jesus to not be "afraid, but speak and hold not your peace," while witnessing to the people of Corinth. And just like Paul, I followed Jesus' command and with His strength, I spoke to my friends about salvation. They no longer consider me to be their friend but they now know that Jesus can save them and that I am praying for them. *(Pause)* World, you Caused me to Pause in making me Jump away from Jesus. And if I am going to continue to stay close to Jesus and walk the path of righteousness, I must determine to what height that I will Jump for others.

(JUMPER exits. Three seconds later, ENVY enters.)

ENVY: You—the World Caused me to Pause because I became so Envious of what other people had, especially the things that my unsaved friends owned. That is why I believe that Psalm 73:3, was written just for me, because it says, "I was envious …when I saw the prosperity of the wicked." *(Pause then point to self.)* I was constantly thinking, "Why can't I have the face and body of a model, the hottest outfits, and the cutest boyfriend? Why can't I be one of the popular kids that others want to hang around with? Why can't my parents make enough money so that I can buy things like the rich kids? *(Bring hand down.)* I am telling you that the sin of Envy had wrapped itself around me so comfortable, I could not see straight. Not only was I envious, I also became seriously upset that I couldn't be or have those things. *(Pause)* Mercifully, the Holy Spirit opened my eyes and un-wrapped the cloak of Envy that was becoming tighter and tighter around me. *(Point toward audience.)* Hear me when I say, please do not lust after what others may have because some things are not meant for you to have. *(Bring hand down.)* Mainly because for one, you may not be mentally ready to receive that blessing from God. Or two, that which you desire or lust after, could have a bad effect on your life. *(Pause)* World, you Caused me to Pause because I was so tied up in the sin of Envy that it almost destroyed me. Now with the Holy Spirit's help, I am able to love who I am, what I look like and to discern what is temporary in this earthly life of mine and what is eternal.

(ENVY exits. Three seconds later, SOLOIST 2 and CHOIR will enter together and sing, "Be Strong in the Lord," then exit. Four seconds later, SPEAKER 4 enters.)

SPEAKER 4: Too many people take their problems, pains and heartaches to other people so that others may listen, help them and/or fix whatever it is that needs fixing. I say why not take whatever you need to talk about or need fixing to the Father of us all and His Son Jesus Christ. If you get to know God the Father, His Son Jesus and the Holy Spirit in a personal way, you can talk and fellowship with Them, anytime, day or night. The Holy Bible says "Blessed is every one that feareth the Lord; that walketh in his ways." If your fear of the Lord God is greater than anything on this earth, then you will not be swayed by anything detriment to your mental or physical condition. If you allow emotion, sin and other distractions to take over your everyday thoughts and actions, you will miss out on some of the awe-inspiring things that Jesus may say to you and/or do for you. The Bible also says that "A double minded man is unstable in all his ways." Therefore, we all should take some time, get in a quiet place and clear our mind. Then we should refocus on what is important in our lives and discard everything that causes worry, stress, drama and anxiety in our lives.

(SPEAKER 4 exits. Three seconds later, ANGRY enters.)

ANGRY: You—the World Caused me to Pause because I became so Angry with what one of my classmates did to me that I was on the verge of considering doing something criminal to him. Long story short, he set me up so that he and others could laugh at me in front of the entire class. *(Point toward audience.)* I am telling that person here and now, that I am not like you and I pray that you remember at least the words of the Golden Rule before you decide to hurt someone else. *(Bring hand down.)* Just because I do not disrespect people like you do, does not mean that I am a pushover. *(Pause)* Payback? Yes, I thought about it for a long while. *(Raise palm toward audience.)* But I was taught to pray for my enemies and the Lord's "commandments hast made me wiser than mine enemies…." *(Bring hand down.)* Furthermore, my Lord and Savior, Jesus Christ would not be honored if I did anything as an act of vengeance. *(Point toward audience.)* So to the one who pulled that prank on me, I know for a fact that you are not so mentally secure as you want your friends to think. *(Bring hand down.)* I could do something to you that would shame you so bad that I know you would not mentally recover from it. You forget that most teenagers are controlled mentally by social media. A click here, a click there, a post or picture can damage a person's mental stability and their reputation for life. To the World and to that person, I want you to know, I will not Pause my life for this intrusion on my mental well being. I will strive to be someone who is a friend not to some social media site but to someone who is standing near or around me. *(Pause)* World, you may have Caused me to Pause but I will not become Angry or mentally unstable over these earthly circumstances to the point of revenge. For my God and Savior Jesus Christ has made me stronger than all of that.

(ANGRY exits. Three seconds later, CONFUSED enters.)

CONFUSED: You—the World Caused me to Pause because I became Confused. *(Pause)* I thought once I became a teenager, that I would understand everything that I needed to. I really believed that I had stepped onto the planet called, 'Comprehension of Life.' I was so sure that I knew everything that I needed to know about the ways of the world. So much so, that I believed that I didn't need anyone, especially my parents, to tell me what was right or wrong. I quickly found that as a teenager, I was not as knowledgeable as I thought. Later, as the years went by, I even fooled myself in thinking that everyone would like me as a hard headed rebel. I can tell you, without going into details that there were too many lessons learned. *(Pause)* Most of them learnt the hard way and others in a painful way. I can tell you that those lessons became vital points that I keep for future reference. In truth, I knew that I would be wasting my time trying to blame God because "God is not the author of confusion, but of peace…." So, when I finally stepped from under that cloud of Confusion, I got to thinking straight. First, I apologized to God and the Lord Jesus Christ and asked Them to forgive me. Then I apologized to my parents and others for all the disappointments, pain and worry that *(Point to self.)* I Caused them. *(Bring hand down.)* With the help of the Holy Spirit and my parents I will strive to not go back to doing the stupid things I used to do. *(Pause)* World, you Caused me to Pause because in my mental Confusion, I thought that I was an all-knowing Teenager. I have learned to no longer act as though I am God and I will now eagerly listen to godly counsel from the Holy Spirit, my parents, grandparents and my fellow Christians.

(Three seconds after CONFUSED exits, turn off all Stage lights. Four seconds later, in front of the mikes, turn on Spotlights at center Stage.

After five seconds, from the Entrance, NURSE and NURSE 2 will roll in front of the mikes, 'the Machines' to center Stage into the Spotlights.

As LPN and LPN 2 roll in hospital bed with YOUTH to center Stage in front of 'the Machines.' LPN will pull the bed and LPN 2 will be pushing the bed.

After both LPNs roll YOUTH into place, they will exit through the Entrance as NURSE begins to check 'the Machines' cords or lines attached to the bed.

When NURSE is finished, play S-Recording #1 and #2. NURSE 2 will begin to adjust items on IV poles while NURSE 'checks the Patient' and adjusts the blanket on the bed.

While they are doing all that, NURSE 3 enters carrying the Patient chart. She is writing something on the chart. NURSE exits.

The Recordings are still playing. NURSE 2 continues to 'check Patient' and NURSE 3 moves to look at 'the Machines' monitors and write.

Seven seconds later, NURSE 2 exits and NURSE 3 finishes up with notes, looks over Patient again, place the chart on the bed and exit.

Three seconds later, turn down Recordings #1 and #2 enough so that they are heard but lower than YDR. Once S-Recordings #1 and #2 are lowered, play YDR.)

YOUTH: You—the World Caused me to Pause because I tried to commit suicide. I came to the point of ending my life but fate would have it, someone stopped me in time. *(Pause)* Why would I do such a thing, you may ask? *(Pause)* Well, I could blame myself but most people do not do that. They say that it is easier to blame someone or something else for your unhappy circumstances, your bad behavior, your helpless predicaments or bad decisions. So that is what I will do at this time. I blame my *(Pause)* existing condition on others because I jumped whenever those who I wanted as friends asked me to. Why? *(Pause)* Because, I desperately wanted to be friends with them or any other popular group of friends. Also, I became envious of classmates who were attractive, who wore the newest style clothing and always had money to spend. This Caused me to become miserable, because I could not be like them nor have the things that they had. Deep down,

I now know that it would not have mattered if I had the beauty, the money, or hundred of friends because my ego is such that I would not have gotten enough of each one to be satisfied. All the same, the blame still should not fall on me. *(Pause)* I blame others when I felt betrayed after I confessed a secret to friends who I thought would keep it. And the time when I became really angry with some of my classmates because they would not let me join them when they went and spent all day out of town together. When I think about it, at the top of my Blame list, should be the time when I cried constantly because Jenny, the girl I love, dumped me. I thought that she really cared about me. I found out that she was pretending to like me so that I would fall in love with her, which I did. Plus, she wanted to have a guy to give her gifts and follow her around like a puppy like her best friends' boyfriends do. *(Pause)* Jenny played with my emotions, just to win the bet that she could make me love her and turned me into her puppy boyfriend. *(Pause)* The hurt was deep and painful and in spite of my heartache, I still feel that she would have been the wife I dream of having. *(Pause for four seconds.)* I could blame my situation on the day I became a teenager and thought that I would know how to turn myself into this person who everyone would want to hang around with. I was both frustrated and confused for two years. *(Pause)* Then I ran. I ran around trying to be like the popular guys and chased after a lot of girls or anything else that I thought would make me well liked. And like everyone else, I too, wanted the newest electronic or video gadgets whether I could afford them or not. I burned in the desire to possess them no matter what it took to get them. *(Pause)* I also throw blame toward others when, I thought I could handle my social and psychologically anxieties by drinking and using drugs. Which did not work! Then I became so tired of trying to be what I know I was not, that I emotionally bottomed out. That's when I decided that committing suicide was the answer to the question of 'How can I get rid of all of my troubles?' *(Pause)* How stupid of me, I could have died! *(Pause)* Then what? Where would I have gone? *(Pause for four seconds.)* I heard about heaven and Hell from one of the church-going guys at my school, but I made fun of him, like everyone else did. *(Pause)* If I get out of this hospital bed, I will find that guy and let him tell me about this Jesus and the God who supposed to love us no matter what we have done. *(Start crying for four seconds then speak the rest of your lines.)* I want to live! I want to live! Please, *(Pause)* if there is a merciful God in heaven, please help me to live! I want my life back! Please help me!

(Immediately after YOUTH finishes the last words of the YDR, turn off S-Recording #1 and #2.

At the same time, turn on S-Recording #3. Three seconds later, NURSE 2 and NURSE rush on Stage.

NURSE 2 'checks Patient' as NURSE stands by and checks 'the Machines.' Continue to play S-Recording #3. NURSE 2 turns and looks at NURSE then speaks.)

NURSE 2: He seems to be fine now. You can reset the machine.

(NURSE nods okay while working on 'the Machines.' NURSE 2 moves to get the chart. Three seconds later, turn off S-Recording #3.

Immediately turn S-Recordings #1 and #2 back on but at a lower volume so that the audience can hear the Nurses speaking. NURSE 3 enters.)

NURSE 3: I got a call, is everything okay?

NURSE 2: Yes. *(Hand chart to NURSE 3 as NURSE moves near you.)*

NURSE: It was only the machine.

(NURSE looks at NURSE 3, who is looking at chart. NURSE 2 is glancing at the Patient and 'the Machines.')

NURSE 3: Okay. You know what? Let's take him down to Room 20. It's cleaned and empty now.

NURSE: Great! That room has more space for the family to visit. *(Move over to 'the Machines.')*

NURSE 3: We'll move everything there. *(Place chart on bed slot and remain in place as NURSE exits.)*

(Three seconds later, both LPNs enter. They will roll 'the Machines' out as all three Nurses roll the bed toward the Entrance and exit.

Continue to play S-Recording #1 and #2, until 'the Machines'; the Nurses and YOUTH are off Stage.

Three seconds later, turn off all Recordings. Four seconds later, U-SPEAKER and U-SPEAKER 2 will speak.)

U-SPEAKER: The Clock Is Ticking! Repent Now! While There is Time!

U-SPEAKER 2: Your life is precious to your loved ones, your friends and most of all to God the Father, the One who gave you the breath of life!

U-SPEAKER: Don't give up on life! Don't be afraid to live your life, no matter the circumstances!

U-SPEAKER 2: You can make it! *(Pause)* Mostly because many people before you have entered into, went through and came out of different situations that have affected their lives.

U-SPEAKER: Even today, there are those young or old who are physically and mentally making it through all types of difficulties that life has thrown their way.

U-SPEAKER 2: And day by day in all those difficulties, they keep looking forward to the next day. If they can do it, *(Pause)* you can too!

U-SPEAKER: So live the life you were given because tomorrow is another day.

U-SPEAKER 2: And we pray that you feel blessed and strong enough to live to see it!

(Four seconds after U-SPEAKER and U-SPEAKER 2 finishes, TIRED will enter.)

TIRED: You—the World Caused me to Pause because I was so Tired of trying to be what I was not. Not only am I a nerd but I am a Christian too. *(Pause)* Every time, I left my house, I would put on an act of being this worldly person. Since I wanted to be just like some of the teenagers who were well known and liked in school, I pretended to be okay with their worldly behavior and beliefs. Thinking that they would not accept me as I am, I pretended that I was just as worldly as they were. Plus, I mimicked their anti-this or anti-that speech. *(Pause)* I hate to say it but I went along with these friends of mine as they teased and laughed at other teenagers who I knew were just like me but those teenagers chose to be themselves. Sad to say, I was a coward and a silent Christian just like some of the other young people I see in the community. *(Pause)* However, it has been proven over and over that the Lord Jesus will not leave you where He found you. Jesus wants His followers to always be about growing spiritually and moving along the path of righteousness. The Holy Scriptures says that "they that wait upon the Lord shall renew their strength…they shall run, and not be weary; and they shall walk, and not faint." I have that strength now and I am learning to be myself and to fulfill whatever purpose God has for me. I no longer pretend to be one of the crowds. I am showing others that I have morals, that I have compassion and most importantly, that I am a Christian teenager. *(Pause)* World, you Caused me to Pause because I became so Tired of being a silent Christian, that I was weary to the point of spiritually exhaustion. And World, you tried and failed to prevent me from standing for my Lord Jesus and obtaining the heavenly prize of eternal life with Him and the Father.

(TIRED exits. Three seconds later, JOY enters.)

JOY: You—the World Caused me to Pause because of its constant laughter at my enthusiasm and Joy of living a Christian life. I stopped expressing my enthusiasm at finding out what the Lord Jesus has directed me to do with my life. At the time, I did not realize that certain people around me had no ambition, no purpose, no joy in their life, so they sought to destroy my joyfulness in Jesus. It seems as if it is getting to be a daily thing for people to make jokes or talk crudely about Jesus and Christians. Why is it, in our day, are there so many people making it so problematical to believe in and worship Christ Jesus? We Christians are tolerant of others, why can't others be tolerant of us? *(Fold hands as in prayer.)* I daily pray to Jesus the words of Psalm 51:12, which say, "Restore unto me the joy of thy salvation; and uphold me with thy free spirit." So now with the strength of the Spirit of God, I grow stronger and stronger in my faith and love for my Lord and Savior. *(Unfold hands.)* Harassing insults and mockery toward me as a Christian are a waste of anyone's time. *(Point to self.)* I have Jesus and with his guidance I know my purpose in life and no other power in the universe can keep me from my destiny. *(Bring hand down.)* To the worldly people around me, I say to you, your refusal to believe in the Lord Jesus and what He has called me to do will not deter me any longer. Nor will your verbal attack against me, discourage my faith in Christ. *(Pause)* World, you Caused me to Pause because I was starting to feel very sad about living the Christian life. Now with my Joy renewed, I pray for all Christians to be encouraged by the Holy Spirit and to joyfully make every effort to fulfill their earthly and spiritually destinies.

(Three seconds after JOY exits, SOLOIST 3 and CHOIR will enter together and sing, "Only Trust Him," then exit.

Four seconds afterward, GUARD will enter from Exit and go and stand in front of the Entrance.

Once in place, GUARD 2 will enter from the Exit, pulling T-PRISONER on Stage.

After GUARD 2 gets T-PRISONER in front of mikes, he will go and stand in front of the Exit. All the while T-PRISONER is looking at GUARD 2.

Once GUARD 2 is in place, T-PRISONER will turn and face audience, give a heavy shrug then begin his dialogue.)

T-PRISONER: You—the World Caused me to Pause because I wanted to be like the teenagers in the gang movies. I thought that they were cool and even though I was a Christian, I wanted to be someone bad. To my family and friends, I was this good kid but in secret, I watched or read anything that has to do with being a bad boy. I even bought some gang related clothing and hid them in my closet. When my chance came to hang with the bad boys, I took it. As I secretly met with them, I was pulled deeper and deeper into their way of thinking. Then the unthinkable happened. One day when one of them offered me a gun, I gladly took it and hid it in my room. A couple of weeks later, I lied to my parents and said that one of the guys in my Sunday school class had invited over to his house. In my deceit, I meet up with my boys downtown. They showed me the masks that they had made for us to use. Then they told me that the five of us were going to break into this rich guy's house. I was scared when our leader, Ralph said that this was not his first break-in. Ralph said that the rich guy was out of town and he heard that the guy always had money and jewelry lying out in the open. Ralph also said that it would be an easy in and out operation. The thought of making an excuse and leaving did not pop into my head. All I thought about was finding enough money to get this cool watch that my Dad said was too expensive for me to have. *(Pause)* Well, to make a long story short, we thought that the rich guy had forgot to lock the side door near the pool. While we were stealing stuff from the room near the pool, we found out that he was n-o-t out of town. He came down with his gun and we all got into a shoot-out. Ralph, our so-called leader took off and left the rest of us to suffer the consequences. As a result, the four of us got shot at least two times. Two of my cool friends were killed and I and the other one survived our wounds. My parents, brothers, sisters and our church were all shocked to say the least. Now I am serving time for my foolishness. All I can say is that I sinned against my Lord for deliberately doing something I knew to be wrong. I also sinned against my family and my fellow Christians, especially those in our church. Our Pastor had always preached that we often are not tempted and then commit sin in that moment but many times we are tempted and we gradually feed that temptation and it becomes an act of sin. *(Pause then hold up your arms showing shackles.)* Of which I am proof. So as I stand before you, in these shackles, I am asking that you fellow teenagers, especially those who are Christians, to not ignore any moral teaching and to not let your spiritual guard down because you will wind up like me. *(Pause)* Even though I am in prison, I give thanks to Jesus that I survived and was able to ask Him to forgive me for my sinful decisions and act of rebelliousness. And I also asked Him to forgive me for n-o-t witnessing to m-y boys before that fateful and tragic night. *(Shake head sadly.)* A missed opportunity *(Pause)* that I will regret for the rest of my life. *(Pause)* World—you Caused me to Pause because you enticed me to be someone I thought was cool. *(Pause then turn to GUARD 2.)* I am ready to go now.

(GUARD 2 moves and takes T-PRISONER back through Exit as GUARD follows.

Four seconds later, SPEAKER 5 and SPEAKER 6 will enter together.)

SPEAKER 5: From the cradle to the years of confusion, hormone intensity, emotional awakening and the continue fear of becoming an outsider, the world of a Teenager is a very complex environment.

SPEAKER 6: Ever since Adam and Eve begin to have children, millions upon billions of teenagers have entered this phase of life and came out of it into the world of adulthood.

SPEAKER 5: Unfortunately, millions and millions others do not enjoys the wonderment, the fascination of physical and mental changes and the opportunities to do more and more grown-up things.

SPEAKER 6: Sadly, they do not survive the pressures and pains of life during this time. An even sadder fact, is that they choose to end it all themselves.

SPEAKER 5: As the World, you will cause all of us to Pause for we all live on this earth. But the grace and mercy of the Father, His Son, Jesus Christ and the Holy Spirit can help us *(Slowly speak the last part of this sentence.)* to avoid letting life keep us in a tempting, sinful or confused moment.

SPEAKER 6: With Jesus as our Lord and Savior, we should only Pause when we come in conflict with what the Holy Bible tells us and what the world wants us to do. Jesus said that we are in the World but He did not want us to become what the World is about.

SPEAKER 5: We pray that all of you wake up and stay as close to Jesus as you can. And please be watchful in how far you move away from the foot of the Cross.

SPEAKER 6: Because if you stray too far, the things of this World will Cause you to Pause, and you may never recover from that state of immobility.

(All SPEAKERS exit together. Three seconds later, DESIRE enters carrying two of the three Prop devices.)

DESIRE: You—the World Caused me to Pause because I Desired *(Hold up the devices then bring them back down to your sides.)* like some of my friends the newest electronic gadgets that are out there. I didn't care how I got them—as long as I got them. *(Look at them then back at audience.)* After I had them for a while, I realized how they were causing me to become socially isolated and to the point of creating my own little dream world. Even though I had all these friends online, I really didn't have many that I could hang out with or talk face to face with. *(Hold devices up again.)* These gadgets had me spending so much of my time doing trivial stuff that I failed to take care of myself or to interact with those in my family. I also neglected my spiritual responsibilities. *(Bring them back down.)* As I looked at others around me, they too, were isolating themselves. *(Pause)* Some, to the beginning point of forgetting what reality meant, were going down the same road that I was traveling on. *(Pause)* While others had reached their destination of mentally living in a fantasy world. That is why I am grateful to the Holy Spirit for stepping in and helping me to let go of the attractiveness *(Hold devices up again.)* that I had for these things. Jesus said that we all should "desire spiritually gifts" instead of material things. *(Bring them back down then Pause.)* I should have remembered that! *(Pause)* World, you Caused me to Pause because of my Desire for material things. Well, I am done with being consumed with obtaining the latest things and living in an isolated and dream world. I am getting out of this electronic seclusion and returning to personal and social contact with others. Moreover, I am going back to the forgiveness of Calvary's Cross and the close fellowship of being with my Lord and Savior, Jesus Christ.

(DESIRE exits. Three seconds later, POPULAR enters.)

POPULAR: You—the World Caused me to Pause because I wanted desperately to be Popular like so many of my classmates. To be the cutest and most sought after girl in school is what I came to believe was my life's goal. I cannot believe that I wasted so much time and energy trying to be the center of attention. I am so glad that the Holy Spirit woke me up from that illusion. In the Bible, Jesus said, "For what is a man profited, if he shall gain the whole world and lose his own soul? or what shall a man give in exchange for his soul?" I know, *(Pause)* it is shameful what we are willing to do in order to be among those who are well-liked and exclusive. Do you know that when I became Ms. Popularity, I was really miserable? The constant stealing of my time, personal and socially, almost Caused me to have a nervous breakdown. *(Point toward audience.)* I say to my fellow teenagers, you may think that you want to be Popular *(Pause)* but it is not as great as you dream it to be. *(Bring hand down.)* Trying to do everything the World wants you to do so that you are greatly accepted, trust me it is not a good thing to do, especially if you are a Christian. Because you w-i-l-l at one point stop letting the World know that you believe in Jesus, to the point of acting as though you do not know anything about Him. In the Book of James, it asks, "know ye not that the friendship of the world is enmity with God? It also says that "whosoever therefore will be a friend of the world is the enemy of God." *(Pause)* I want to thank the Holy Spirit for opening my eyes to the dangers of being too acceptable and admired. Now that my eyes are opened, I am no longer consumed with gaining favorable recognition in my school and a higher status among my circle of friends. *(Pause)* World, you Caused me to Pause because I wasted valuable time trying to be and stay *(Pause)* Popular. Nowadays, I hope to help someone else see the error in trying to travel down the Popularity road.

(POPULAR exits and three seconds later, B-TEEN and B-TEEN 2 will enter together.)

B-TEEN: Back in the old days, the explanation that most people gave for committing crimes, misconduct, sin or any other evil *(Pause)* was: "The Devil made me do it."

B-TEEN 2: It was the number one reason given because everyone knows that the Devil is all about making your life miserable.

B-TEEN: And the Devil is all about making you waste your life by doing nothing that will improve your character or fellowship with others.

B-TEEN 2: And most important; he will make sure that you are doing nothing that will cause you to reconcile with God the Father, Jesus Christ and the Holy Spirit.

B-TEEN: The popular thing for a lot of people to do today is to n-o-t take responsibility for anything that they say or do.

B-TEEN 2: The Motto, 'Blame it on someone or something else,' is the motto of too many people.

B-TEEN: We have turned the Blame Game into something that too many of us love to play. And I mean too many of us!

B-TEEN 2: The Blame Game has lot of cards in its deck.

B-TEEN: And young children, teenagers, adults, community and religious leaders, local, state and federal politicians all have access to the Game.

B-TEEN 2: And all have used a card from the deck of the Blame Game.

B-TEEN: Some of the Cards in the deck are: Blame it on an imaginary friend or monster.

B-TEEN 2: Blame it on not having loving parents or the lack of teaching you should have received from your parents.

B-TEEN: Blame it on the place or conditions in which you grew up in.

B-TEEN 2: Blame it on the lack of someone to be there to guide or mentor you in personal or socially relationships.

B-TEEN: Blame it on the lack of material things that you do not have now or didn't have while growing up.

B-TEEN 2: The number one material thing was and still is *(Pause)* the lack of lots of money!

B-TEEN: If you have not played the Blame Game, we ask that you stay away from it.

B-TEEN 2: But if you have played the Blame Game, we ask that you quickly put down the cards.

B-TEEN: Step away from the Blame Game and don't look back!

B-TEEN 2: Be mature and take responsibility for your own words and actions.

B-TEEN: Become Blame free.

B-TEEN 2: And live your life responsibly.

(Both TEENS exit and three seconds later, HURT enters.)

HURT: You—the World Caused me to Pause because of a Hurt and betrayal that were so deep and painful that I considered doing something to someone that would have been very wrong to do. To the person who I considered to be a very close friend, I say to you, that my trust in you and our group fondness for you was genuine. Unfortunately, friendship and loyalty are not a part of your nature. Your betrayal was a shock and surprise to all of us. *(Point toward audience.)* You were Judas among our close knit group. *(Bring hand down.)* Things spoken in private you made public not caring what effect it had on anyone including your friends. We as a Group, thought you were a fellow Christian. A teenager, who was also trying to get through these chaotic times like the rest of us. Now because of your betrayal, everyone in our group is becoming suspicious of each other, wondering if we can trust one another again with our innermost thoughts. The Holy Bible tells us that we as Christians ought to be discerner of people we hang around with but I ignored that spiritual instruction. The Bible also says that a person who "hath friends must shew himself friendly…." *(Pause)* With painful lessons learned, I will now pay better attention to what the Word of God says. Plus, I now talk to Jesus a lot more about what is going on in my life. To Judas, our so-called friend, I pray that you will repent of your sins before the Lord deals with you. And I will also strive to be a better friend to others than you have been to us. *(Pause)* To the World, I say, you have Caused me to Pause because of the Hurtful act and betrayal of a Judas. And I have to tell you World and Judas, that I will no longer be in mental and spiritual pain because the Holy Spirit has touched my heart and mind and eased the pain that had wrapped itself around me. Now, I can continue on the path of righteousness to fulfill the work that Jesus has for me to do before He comes back for me.

(HURT exits and three seconds later, SPEAKER 7 and SPEAKER 8 will enter together.)

SPEAKER 7: Are you feeling lonely, hurt, depressed, worthless, afraid or lost?

SPEAKER 8: Hold On! There is a Friend, a Healer, a Prince of peace, a Defender, a Savior and Redeemer, in the Lord Jesus Christ.

SPEAKER 7: As a Friend, Jesus will always be there for you to talk to and fellowship with.

SPEAKER 8: As a Healer, Jesus can heal your broken heart, soul and body!

SPEAKER 7: As the Prince of peace, Jesus can bring peace to your heart, mind and soul.

SPEAKER 8: As a Defender, Jesus will stand up and defend you before the God the Father.

SPEAKER 7: As a Savior, Jesus is the only One who the Father says can forgive you of your sins and save you from damnation.

SPEAKER 8: As a Redeemer, Jesus has the power to redeem you holy enough to become a Child of the Father.

SPEAKER 7: The Lord Jesus also brings joy, fellowship, grace, love, righteousness and tranquility, all in His powerful and holy Name.

SPEAKER 8: Jesus is King of kings, the Lord of lords and the only begotten Son of God the Father.

SPEAKER 7: Therefore, you have someone else like the Father and the Holy Spirit who is holy enough for you or anyone else, to look up to, praise and worship.

SPEAKER 8: So remember there is love, hope and a future for you in the Lord Jesus Christ!

(Four seconds after SPEAKER 7 and SPEAKER 8 exit, SOLOIST 4 and CHOIR will enter and sing, "In Christ Alone (My Hope Is Found)," then exit together.

Four seconds later, CRIED will enter.)

CRIED: You—the World Caused me to Pause because I Cried constantly because Jeremy, the guy I love and thought the world of *(Pause)* dumped me. In my pain and sorrow, I thought that I would never find another guy like him. My heart and soul ached for months from the disappointment. As I thought about all of the times we spent together, I was hit with the painful fact that I had spent many days and nights thinking and dreaming about Jeremy. Now, I have come to the realization that he never really cared for me. *(Pause)* The Holy Spirit remained me of the verse that says, that "the Spirit of truth…will guide you into all truth…." Tears were shed because I had willingly ignored all the warnings that the Holy Spirit gave me when I first met Jeremy. I also ignored the spiritual hints concerning his speech and behavior. *(Shrug shoulders.)* Yet in my lust, I really thought Jeremy was a good guy. So I now understand that I need to seek the guidance of the Holy Spirit as to who I should give my love and time to. And that I should wait on the Lord Jesus to let me know what guy He has chosen for me to love and one day marry. *(Pause)* World, you Caused me to Pause because I Cried about not having the boyfriend that I wanted. But I know that I no longer have to cry and scream like there is no tomorrow when I am deeply sad or disappointed. I understand that this life is temporary but the love my Lord Jesus has for me is eternal.

(CRIED exits. Three seconds later, FALLEN enters.)

FALLEN: You—the World Caused me to Pause because I Fell down into the chaos that I created. I thought I could handle the mess that I had gotten myself into. Others tried to warn me but I ignored their advice. Some of you may look at me and say that I had fallen on bad luck. Yeah, right! I stand here before you and tell you that I messed up by running away from home and I cannot blame anyone but myself. *(Pause)* All because, I could not wait to go out and experience the world on my own. With the loot of cash I stole from my Daddy's safe, the credit card that he gave me when I was 14 and the burner phone that I had bought months ago, I thought that I was well equipped to fly the nest. Because I wanted to have some fun before they caught up with me, I decided to leave the card because I knew that my parents could track it if I purchased anything. *(Pause for three seconds.)* Hear me when I say, the grown up world does not play by teenager rules. Which, I quickly found out after three months on my own, trying to live off the money I stole from Daddy. *(Point toward audience.)* Young people, you may dream of how wonderful it would be on your own but with no job, no home, no money and under aged, you are a disaster in the making. *(Bring hand down.)* All those music videos and TV shows that I used to watch made it seem so great to be out doing what I thought was fun to do. *(Bump palm against head.)* But dumb old me didn't stop to think that most of those videos and TV shows are fantasy worlds created by rich music and show producers. *(Pause)* When I first took off, I was doing ok but that soon changed. With the people that I met and the things I wound up doing were not pretty. *(Look at bandaged hand then at audience.)* Don't ask! *(Pause)* I know now that I had lost my ever-loving mind when I ran away from a great home life. Being out there homeless, half starved, half dressed, cold and beaten up, *(Hold up foot with cast for two seconds then point to face.)* don't ask, can make you come to your senses real quick. *(Point to tattoo on neck.)* Don't ask, mainly because I still can't remember when or where I got this! *(Point to self.)* I want you to know that this teenager repented and confessed her sins and stupidity to Jesus Christ. Then I prayed and asked Him to "Create in me a clean heart, O God; and renew a right spirit within me." "Purge me…[and] wash me…and blot out all mine iniquities" which were many. *(Bring hand down.)* With the Lord's help, I remembered my Dad once told me, when in trouble, find the police or go to the police station. And that is what I did. Let me tell you, as a saved person, Jesus will forgive you of your sins but you may also suffer the consequences of your stupid actions. *(Extend both arms outward.)* And I am standing here as Exhibit A. *(Pause)* Now that I am at home again, I am working on changing my rebellious attitude and very careful about people that I allow within my inner circle and the things that can have a negative influence in my life. It may be popular for you to n-o-t take responsibility for anything that you may do wrong but 'Blaming someone else,' is not my motto. I also have to own up to the sins that I have committed and will commit in the future. *(Pause)* I am here to say, *(Pause)* World, you Caused me to Pause because I thought I was grown up enough to handle my business. *(Pause)* I couldn't! To tell the truth, I really didn't know what my business was. *(Pause)* Nevertheless, I know now that I don't have to stay down when I Fall down.

(FALLEN exits and three seconds later, RAN enters.)

RAN: You—the World Caused me to Pause because I Ran. *(Pause)* I ran around trying to be like other guys and chased after every girl I could get. Yes, I know as a Christian, I should have been more disciplined in my personal conduct than the other guys but there are so many pretty girls out there. And during that time, the Holy Spirit was wearing my conscious out to stop me from sinning all over town. Finally, I had to stop and take a hard look at the hypocrisy I was wrapped in. I wanted to be like the rest of the World and be in Christ at the same time. Thank you Holy Spirit for waking me up to the spiritual damage that I was causing to my faith in Jesus and the sexual and social turmoil I was causing to others. I am so thankful that I was stopped before I became a disgrace to my Lord Jesus, my parents and myself. *(Point to self.)* I prayed for the Lord Jesus, "to blot out my transgressions" and to "Wash me thoroughly from mine iniquity" so that He could "cleanse me from my sin." I have rededicated my life to the Lord Jesus Christ and submitted to His will for my life. *(Bring hand down.)* I know now if I try to go my own way, I will take myself and maybe others down a depraved and destructive path. *(Pause)* World, you Caused me to Pause because I willingly Ran to get into sinful behavior. Fortunately, I have learned my lesson and I pray that I will not back away from what I know to be right. With the blessing of Jesus, I will walk slowly and sure-footed on the path that He has laid out before me.

(RAN exits. Three seconds later, LONELY enters.)

LONELY: You—the World Caused me to Pause because I got so Lonely after I confessed to my friends that I had accepted Jesus Christ as my Lord and Savior. Afterward, they started avoiding me once they realized that I was a Christian and all about Jesus. They decided to no longer hang out with me or speak to me. I went through a sad and lonely phase until one night, the Holy Spirit of God spoke to my heart. The next morning, I found out that I had this inner strength and courage to walk alone among my used-to be friends without being ashamed of believing in Jesus and walking the path of righteousness. To my surprise, I felt relieved. *(Pause)* Relieved, that I no longer had to hide my faith. *(Pause)* So if you find yourself feeling lonely, kneel down and talked to Jesus. He will always be there to listen to you. You can talk to Jesus about your hopes, your dreams, your disappointments, heartaches and about other things that affect you. The

Lord Jesus can give you that sense of belonging and being loved. For he said in the Book of Matthew, "lo, I am with you alway, even unto the end of the world." *(Pause)* So World, you Caused me to Pause because I was so Lonely but I soon remembered that I have the love and the companionship of Jesus Christ, my Savior to sustain me. Plus, I now know that Jesus will bring others along my life's path who will become my new friends.

(LONELY exits. Four seconds later, U-SPEAKER 3 and U-SPEAKER 4 will speak.)

U-SPEAKER 3: Your life is precious to God the Father, the Lord Jesus Christ and the Holy Spirit!

U-SPEAKER 4: So much so, that Jesus allowed Himself to be falsely accused, sentenced, beaten and scourged.

U-SPEAKER 3: God the Father also willingly allowed His only Son, Jesus to go through all of that, along with the suffering and agony of being nailed and hung on a cross to die.

U-SPEAKER 4: This sacrifice of the Holy Son of God was so that Jesus could shed His blood to cover anyone who wanted to be redeemed from their sins.

U-SPEAKER 3: You have to be redeemed from your sins in order to become holy enough to join the heavenly family of God the Father.

U-SPEAKER 4: With the Father, Jesus Christ, the Holy Spirit and the rest of the heavenly host, you will live together forever!

(Four seconds after U-SPEAKER 3 and U-SPEAKER 4 finishes, turn off all Stage lights.

After three seconds turn Spotlight(s) on center Stage.

Three seconds later, LPN will bring in the Chair; place it in front of the mikes but out of the Spotlights then exit.

Both LPNs will roll the other machines in into the Spotlights as NURSE 2 pulls and NURSE 2 push the hospital bed with YOUTH 2 into the Spotlights in front of 'the machines.'

NURSE 3 enters carrying and looking at the chart. Both LPNS will exit.

NURSE will 'check the Patient,' adjust the IV pole and the blanket on the rear side.

NURSE 2 is at 'the machines' checking them.

Play S-Recordings #2 and #4. Remember to lower volume enough for audience to hear the Nurses speak.

NURSE 3, still looking at the chart, will be standing three steps from NURSE near the knees of YOUTH 2.

When NURSE 2 speaks, NURSE 3 will turn to face him.

NURSE 2: Her Mom and one of her brothers each gave a pint of blood if she needs it.

NURSE 3: I will note it on the chart.

(NURSE 3 writes on the chart as she moves to the foot of the bed. Four seconds later, as she is folding the flap of the chart, she looks up at YOUTH 2 for two seconds.

She notices the blood stain, (½ of an inch in diameter) on YOUTH 2's head bandages that is facing the audience.

Laying the chart at the feet of YOUTH 2, she goes and checks it.)

NURSE 3: Her head wound is bleeding again but not as bad as it once did.

(NURSE 2 moves near NURSE.)

NURSE 2: I'll notify the doctor that he may have to examine the wound again.

NURSE 3: We'll keep watch on the stain.

(NURSE 2 rushes off Stage as NURSE 3 moves back to the foot of bed and picks up the chart and start writing on it again.

NURSE goes over to 'the machines' checking them. NURSE 3 remains in place. NURSE looks at NURSE 3 then speaks.)

NURSE: I pray that she pulls through.

NURSE 3: Yes, so do I! The wound is really bad.

NURSE: It's sad when things get so bad in your life…. *(Slowly shake your head back and forth as though you are sad.)*

NURSE 3: I know. It's even sadder because this is not the first or the sixth one we have seen this year. *(Pause for four seconds.)* I'll stay here, so you can go check on Mrs. Kay.

(NURSE quickly exits and NURSE 3 places the chart in the slot then go out of the Spotlight(s) to sit in the chair.

After she has been sitting for five seconds, play YDR 2. S-Recordings #2 and #4 are still playing but at lower volume.

PM will move and stand off Stage to be ready to roll Covering Partitions back into place.

Also, the SR Operators must be ready to turn on S-Recording #3 as YOUTH 2 is finishing her last scream.)

YOUTH 2: Here I am lying in this hospital bed because You—the World Caused me to Pause. Like others who tried to commit suicide and were rescued, I was not so lucky. There was no one around to stop me in time. The deed is done and of all the things I have failed at in my life, why didn't I fail at this. *(Pause)* I know that I don't have a lot of time left because I heard the doctors talking. So I want to go out with the realization that I have made a big, big, big mistake. I can't believe that I allowed so many petty things to so affect my life that I thought killing myself would be a good idea. I realize now, that worshipping at the altar of social media and learning all of the ways that I could pay respect to it, I doomed myself. If I was not tweeting, messaging, texting, posting and clicking for hours on end, I was not happy. The World of the Internet embraced me and I fell victim to it in such a way that I believed everything that I received by way of it. *(Pause)* I would not listen to my Mom, Dad, Grandpa, Grandma, my two friends and others who tried to get me to interact with them more. I thought I had a created my own little world in which I could be greatly recognized and loved no matter what. Then when the hateful and malicious words and images came into my world, I could not deal with them. Foolishly, I did not talk to anyone, including my parents about the pain of it all. All I could think of, was that the world that I had created for myself was destroyed and I did not want to exist anywhere else. *(Pause for four seconds. Now voice is sadder.)* I heard Mom, Dad, Stasha, Robert and Jimmy screaming and crying when they found me. Why didn't I take the time to think about how much pain I would cause them? Why didn't I care and understand how precious life is? I guess being self-centered is something my generation strives on. Now, I am at the end of it and no one can help me. Mom and Dad tried to tell me how much they loved me so many times. They even tried several methods of interventions to include having our Pastor talk to me to help me understand that I needed to live in the real world. When they and the Pastor tried to talk to me about Jesus and His love for me, I pretended to listen and to go along with their wishes for me to become a follower of Jesus. On the outside, I pretended to be a Christian but in my heart; I rejected Jesus and His free gift of salvation. Even though I did not believe in Jesus to save me from my sins, I think that He could have stepped in to help me out of my hurt and pain. They say that Jesus has all this power and isn't He a God of love? Therefore, I blame Jesus for not doing anything to stop me from shooting myself. *(Pause)*, I guess I will have to take my chances with whoever else is up there in heaven. *(Pause)* Oh well, I guess it does not matter now, cause I will soon be in a better place. There I will have no more heartache, pain, worries or problems. No more of anything! *(Pause for three seconds then speak in a panic voice.)* Wait! Why is it getting so dark? *(Pause)* What! What are you? *(Pause then scream one time.)* Why is this horrible thing pulling on me? *(Scream two times.)* Let go of me! *(Pause)* Somebody help me! Where did this fire come from? *(Pause)* Please help me, I am burning! *(Pause)* H-e-l-p! *(Scream two more times.)*

(Immediately play S-Recording #3. NURSE 3 quickly stands up and goes to examine YOUTH 2. Play S-Recording #5.

Three seconds later, NURSE 2 rushes in and goes to the 'the Machines.'

NURSE 3 is still examining Youth 2, as DOCTOR and NURSE rush in.

NURSE 3 moves aside as DOCTOR checks YOUTH 2, while NURSE 2 rolls over the Defibrillator.

At the same time, NURSE 3 goes to the front side of the bed and stands in-between YOUTH 2's chest and head.

NURSE stands near the IV pole. S-Recording #5 is still playing as S-Recording #3 is turned off. DOCTOR grabs the paddles.)

DOCTOR: Stand clear!

(DOCTOR places the paddles on YOUTH 2's chest. Play S-Recording #6. YOUTH 2's will make the motion of being shocked. S-Recording #5 is still playing.)

DOCTOR: Again!

(DOCTOR places the paddles on YOUTH 2's chest again. Play S-Recording #6. Again, YOUTH 2's will make the motion of being shocked.

S-Recording #5 is still playing. DOCTOR will do whatever it is that is done after shocking a Patient.

While he is doing that, PM will quickly move to roll Covering Partitions back into place. S-Recording #5 is still playing.

PM exits. Five seconds after the Covering Partitions are in place, slowly fade spotlights to black as S-Recording #5 slowly fades and is turned off.

Behind the Covering, Medical Cast members will quietly roll the bed and machines off Stage.

10 seconds later, SPEAKER 9, SPEAKER 10 and SPEAKER 11 will enter together, stand in front of the Covering then speak.)

SPEAKER 9: If you are very young, old or in between, there is always that chance that you may die at any moment.

SPEAKER 10: Whether you are ready to leave this world or not, there is a place that your soul will live out eternity.

SPEAKER 11: The Holy Bible lets us know that no matter how we died, where we died or when we died, everyone will be resurrected from the dead.

SPEAKER 9: If you are alive when the Rapture comes and you are saved by Jesus, then you will be caught up to meet Him in the clouds.

SPEAKER 10: There with anyone else who has died in righteousness, you will receive your redeemed and new body for your soul to live in. Then Jesus will take you body and soul to heaven.

SPEAKER 11: Everyone else on earth at that time, will go through the horrible years of what is called Tribulation or the Great Tribulation.

SPEAKER 9: In the Book of Revelation, it tells how people still will not repent or believe in or come to Jesus even during those horrifying times.

SPEAKER 10: We just want you to know that whatever you are going through now will pale to what you may have to go through if you are not taken up by Jesus in the coming near future.

SPEAKER 11: Many people believe that they are spiritually starched because they are rigid in religious doctrine.

SPEAKER 9: Others believe that they are spiritually ironed as being pressed down and straight up sanctified to make themselves good enough to go to heaven.

SPEAKER 10: All because of their own self-righteousness or what a so-called religious leader has told them.

SPEAKER 11: But if they are not forgiven and cleansed by the blood and only the blood of the Lord Jesus Christ then they are unredeemed sinners.

SPEAKER 9: Many times, Jesus taught that those not redeemed by Him will be judged, condemned and tossed body and soul into everlasting darkness.

SPEAKER 10: Where there is a furnace of fire, in which all unredeemed will be weeping and gnashing their teeth in everlasting agony.

SPEAKER 11: Therefore, all Christians should obey the words of the Lord by earnestly praying for those who are unredeemed in this world, especially those under the age of 20.

SPEAKER 9: Also, Christian or not, we all must walk wisely, "Redeeming the time, because the days are evil."

SPEAKER 10: For non-Christians, now is the time to come to repentance, now is the time for salvation.

SPEAKER 11: Nevertheless, our prayers for everyone out there, is that you continue in your laughter, your enthusiasm, your joy of wonderment and your love of living life, especially the Christian life.

(All three SPEAKERS will move behind the mikes as all the previous Cast members except for GREETER, reenter from the Entrance and Exit area and assemble around them.

Afterward, SOLOIST 5 and CHOIR will enter and assemble in front of the already assembled Cast.

Three seconds after they are in position, PASTOR will enter, stand in front of the mikes and speak.)

PASTOR: So, are you Pausing in your decision in what you will do with Jesus, the Son of God? If you are, then you need to stop putting on hold, what you know you have to do. As you have heard, time is not on anyone's side. As human beings, we will die at a set point in time. And we all will be resurrected from the dead. When and how, all depends when and where, Jesus designates. I say when because at the time of the Rapture, Jesus will appear and call His own to Himself. Then all the Redeemed who died earlier, will be taken up with the Redeemed who are alive. At that time, you are guarantee to spend eternity with God the Father and Jesus Christ. All the Unredeemed who die after the

Rapture will spend time in Hell until the millennial reign of King Jesus is over. Jesus will then raise all the unredeemed who missed the Rapture and were not saved during the Tribulation period and everyone who were already in Hell. All unredeemed individuals at that time will stand before Jesus, the Judge who will be sitting on the Great White Throne. This is where, one by one, the unredeemed standing before the Throne will be judged from the things listed in the Book of life and the other Books kept in heaven. After your entire life is reviewed and judged, Final Judgment is pronounced against you. Then Jesus will have His Angels take you and cast you into the utter darkness and the fires of the Lake of Fire and Brimstone. And for all of eternity, you will be where the burning fires never go out and the torment and torture of your mind, body and soul will never stop. Hear me as I tell you, salvation paused is salvation lost. Repent of your sins, believe what God has said about His only begotten Son Jesus and how Jesus can forgive and save you from your sins. Repent now and accept Christ Jesus as your personal Lord and Savior.

(SOLOIST 5, CHOIR and the other Cast members will sing, "Just When I Need Him Most" as the Invitation song as PASTOR moves to his designated spot to receive those who will come.

After PASTOR and others are finished with anyone who comes; GREETER will reenter and close the Program.)

GREETER: Thank you for supporting this Performance and bless you for coming. We hope that you have enjoyed our Program. *(Pause)* And we pray that continued blessings of the Father and the Lord Jesus Christ be on you all, especially to those who desire the righteousness of Christ and seek the truths of God the Father. May Christ Jesus bless and keep you as you travel home. Thanks again.

THE END

ABOUT THE AUTHOR

Bobbie J. Gulley is the author of Christian Plays for Children, Kids, Youth and Adults. She is currently working on Second Editions of several previous published Plays. She also has written other Christian themed Books. Listed below are her published works.

Books of Multi-Plays:
Church Plays for Children, Youth Groups and Adults
I Wonder If…
There's A Lion In The Road

Play Series

The Chronicles of the Salvation Hoodlums	The H & H Trinity	Am I Talking?
Come On Up And Play	Did You Eat Yet?	
The Waiting Zone	The Alphabet	
The Threesomes	The Light	
Holy Contact of the Heavenly Kind	In Thee, I Trust	

Second Editions Plays from the Book, 'Church Plays for Children, Youth Groups and Adults.'

Behold My Child Lord	God I
A-B-C…1-2-3	I Want To Be A Light
A-B-C…X-Y-Z	I Trust
Watering the Seed of Salvation	I, I Trust
Who Am I?	I Am A Fool

Second Editions Plays from the Book, 'I Wonder If…'

The Gospel of Sight	Sing High, Sing Low	**Cause To Pause**
Can You Help Me?	Am I Talking About You?	

Separate Christian Play Book
Burning Awakenings contains the Play, 'The Place of Double Hockey Sticks' and the Poem, titled 'Burning.'

Other Separate Christian Play Books are:
Am I Talking About You Too?; A-B-C…N-O-P; Choose Your King!; Duke on the Couch: The Voice Within; Holy Attributes!; Lord Jesus, I Want To Be… ; May I Come With You?; May I Pray For You?; May I Sing?; Our Father Who Arts!; Our Redeemer Lives; Pull-N And Push-N; The Correct Spelling Of…; The Wake Up Call; This Book!; Train Up!; What's In A Name?; What's Your Gift?

Other Books with Christian themes:
Ramblings: From An Un-Trenched Mind, a Book of 10 Poems.
Edifying Crosswords Z
Edifying Crosswords A
Reason Came Riding… —a Life Story & 10-Part Questionnaire for Youths.
Todman: The Then-One-Day Man
Big Momma & The Clothing Trees